THE ULTIMATE BEGINNER'S GUIDE TO TIME MANAGEMENT

A SIMPLE, PRACTICAL GUIDE TO BOOSTING PRODUCTIVITY, BEATING PROCRASTINATION, AND GETTING MORE DONE THAN YOU EVER THOUGHT POSSIBLE

BY

PAUL ROGERS

Legal Disclaimer

All information contained within this publication represents the view of the author as of the date it was produced. Because the Internet and marketing change frequently, the author has the right to change or update the following information based on new conditions. The author's opinion can also change without notice. The author has done their best to ensure that all information contained in this publication to be accurate and currently up to date, but takes no responsibilities because of changing conditions.

While every attempt has been made to verify the information provided, the author takes no responsibility for errors, omissions or inaccuracies. The author is not liable for any actions that may result from the information contained within this publication. The author shall not be held liable to any party or person for any, indirect, special, incidental, direct or any other consequential damages arising from use of the information contained in this publication. The material is provided "as is" and without warranties.

TABLE OF CONTENTS

TIME: THE WORST WASTE OF ALL

Everybody wastes things; there's no point in arguing that. Even the most careful, the most frugal person will wind up wasting something at some time. With most people, it's not unusual to waste food, gas in the car, and money on all sorts of things.

What would you say is the biggest waste of all? No doubt many things you purchase and never use or don't enjoy the way you thought you would may come to mind. You might waste money on a new cell phone that you no longer find exciting after the first week or on cable channels you never watch. You may waste gas in your car running too many errands when you could have and should have combined them into one. Perhaps you wasted food by not using it before it went bad or by cooking too much and throwing away the leftovers.

But with all the things that get wasted in one's life, probably time is the biggest waste of all. Many people waste time on useless activities that don't really serve their needs or on responsibilities that are not done right the first time. Time can be wasted from sleeping too much, from doing harmful things like overdrinking or using narcotics, and from just plain sitting on the couch watching television.

Often time is wasted, not just because people indulge in activities that could be considered a waste of time, but because of poor time management skills. You might compare this to how people waste money on food because they don't use it before it rots or because they cook too much; if a person had better skills when it came to preparing that food and had the discipline needed to use up the food in the house before shopping for more, they may not see so much go down the garbage disposal. It's not their eating that's the problem in of itself and of course it's not the fault of the food that it rots; it's how the food is prepared and used that creates a waste.

So it is with time management skills.

A person may work and work and work and wonder why they're not getting anything done. They may also honestly feel that they don't indulge in time wasting activities such as watching television or going out with friends to the bar every night. And yet, why are they not accomplishing anything or reaching the goals they once had for themselves?

Usually the problem is learning how to manage one's time and to maximize it for the most effectiveness. Just like learning to cook and manage one's shopping can mean better use of the food in the home with less waste, so learning how to be in control of one's time and one's schedule can mean less time wasted.

Your Allotment Of Time

Have you ever found yourself wishing there were more hours in the day in which you could work? Probably so; most people wish this at one time or another. Between careers, household chores, taking care of children, and wanting a little bit of peace and quiet for yourself, no doubt you've found bedtime arriving too soon on more than one occasion.

But has it ever occurred to you that people all around the earth are equal in the fact that they all get the same amount of time every single day? This may be the one constant that everyone shares! You have 24 hours just like your boss, your neighbor, the President, your favorite celebrity, and oh yes, that person that you admire because they always seem to be getting things done effectively.

Realizing that your time is limited and that you have the same amount of time as everyone else should help you to better understand the importance of effective time management. Why is this? Let's again compare time to money. People that are struggling financially often assume that if they just made a few dollars more than they do today, then they wouldn't be struggling and would have all their bills paid, and would enjoy their life.

Of course there are those that struggle because they truly live in poverty and this is not what we're considering here. The point is that while it's tempting to think that the answer to money problems is to have more money, this isn't always the case. Think of those that have literally millions of dollars to their name and still wind up declaring bankruptcy or facing other serious financial problems. No doubt some celebrity names come to mind. And if these people who are making millions and millions of dollars every year still face money problems, what is the issue?

Obviously the answer is that it's the way they manage their money. Having more money won't help if you spend it on useless items that lose value and if you don't save for the future as well. Those celebrities and others that have plenty of money coming in but who face bankruptcy and foreclosure and these issues have not managed the money they have.

So it is with time. If you had 50 hours in the day or even 100, who is to say that you would accomplish more in that time? If you haven't learned to manage the 24 you're allotted, getting more time probably won't make much difference in maximizing your schedule and achieving your goals.

Once It's Gone...

One big consideration when it comes to wasting time is that once it's gone, it's gone. When you waste money you can earn more, when you waste food you can buy more, and so on. But with time, there is no cycle of it that buys back the time that's lost.

Yes, you will have another 24 hours tomorrow but everyone's life is finite; the 24 hours you've wasted today is being subtracted from the total number of hours you'll have in your life overall. You cannot get those hours back the way you can replenish your bank account when you purchase something useless.

This too is why time is so precious and so valuable. And this is why wasting it is probably one of the worst things a person can do! There is no turning back the clock and there is no way to regain that time that is gone.

Time As An Investment

Another reason to consider how time is just too precious to waste is that it can also be seen as an investment in one's future. The way you spend your time today does have an effect on your circumstances tomorrow. When you set goals and use your time toward achieving them, you can soon find yourself living with the end result of those goals being accomplished.

But if you waste time and let it fritter away, then you have nothing to show for it when tomorrow arrives. There are many ways this can be true; consider a few here:

- When you spend time with your children and family now, you are strengthening family bonds that can last a lifetime. Your relationships will be stronger and everyone will feel closer.

- Investing time in furthering your education can mean more earning power. This may mean a more comfortable lifestyle, a more secure retirement, and the ability to provide for oneself and one's family.

- Spending time today caring for your health may mean less health concerns in the future. This may mean exercising more, taking the time to prepare healthy foods, and things such as these.

There are also many personal goals you no doubt have that mean investing time in order to achieve; if you don't invest that time, you won't have the future you imagine. For instance, suppose you want to adopt a child. This means researching the process, selecting an attorney, preparing your home, and doing whatever else is necessary to be eligible for adoption and to make it happen. If you don't use your time today to work toward that goal, of course it will never just happen!

Considering how time is an investment in your future should also encourage you to learn how to manage it wisely. If you let it slip away, this investment will never pay off. But if you use it to reach your goals for tomorrow, then you're using your investment wisely.

Of course, this is all well and good, but knowing how precious time is doesn't typically force anyone to use it wisely. Just about anyone and everyone wastes time often in their lives. Why is this? And how can you change this? Let's first look at why time is often wasted and then we can move on to addressing how to fix these things.

WHY IS TIME BEING WASTED?

If time is so precious and valuable and so limited, why is it always so wasted today? Why do people fritter it away, refuse to recognize it's value, and fail to learn how to manage it wisely?

The answer will be different for everyone. The habits you have that waste time will be different from the practices someone else has. The reasons you struggle to manage your time will be different from the reasons why your spouse is so disorganized, always late, and never seems to accomplish things either.

Typically however there are some common reasons for time being wasted today, and for poor time management skills. Let's take a closer look at these common reasons and then we can discuss each of them in greater detail.

THE PARETO PRINCIPLE

The Pareto Principle is a philosophy regarding cause and effect; it's also known as the 80/20 rule. It simply states that very often, 80% of the effect comes from 20% of the causes.

As an example of how this principle may work in different circumstances, suppose a person is overweight. Chances are the majority of their problem stems from a few small bad habits they have. In other words, some 80% of their excess body weight is probably there because of 20% of their food choices. Those extra desserts they have or fried foods may make up only

20% of their daily diet, but they can probably account for the majority of their excess weight.

As another example, suppose a family or individual faces financial problems even though they make enough money to support themselves. It may very well be that only a few bad habits when it comes to spending are responsible for the majority of their financial concerns. So, 20% of the things they do with their money are causing some 80% of the problems they have with it.

Let's consider how this principle may apply to time management. No doubt there are many things you must do throughout the day over which you have very little say, and there are many time wasters that are just part of today's world. Standing in line, waiting at red lights, sitting through yet another meeting that your boss conducts just to hear himself talk; these are time wasters but they're a part of today's life. To get where we want to go, to buy the food and other things we need, to have a job and earn money, we must simply suffer through these things.

However, when it comes to choices you make about your own time, no doubt it's just a small handful of bad habits or a slight bit of mismanagement that accounts for the majority of the wasted time in your life.

Consider how this might be true. Just two hours of television every night adds up to 14 hours every week that's wasted. That's almost the same amount of hours you spend during two days at work! One afternoon of running all over time to take care of errands that you haven't organized into a quick trip can mean just about your entire day wasted, as you may then be too tired to do anything else at the end of the day.

Very often small habits and small time wasters can add up to hours, days, weeks, and then years being wasted away. The key is to identify those habits and then take steps to address them properly!

PROCRASTINATION

One common element when it comes to wasting time is procrastination. We put off and put off those unpleasant tasks or the work that's needed to accomplish our goals for as long as possible. In some cases this might mean that eventually a situation takes care of itself but rarely is that the case. More often than not we create more problems for ourselves when we put off work or whatever else is necessary in our circumstances.

One reason that procrastination is such a time waster is that the time is sitting right there in front of us, but we do nothing with it. Rather than use it to accomplish our goals we just let it slip away. As said, once it's gone, it's gone for good. Additionally, procrastinating doesn't always make the problem go away. We still need to balance the checkbook and get ourselves on track financially, get that education, find a new job, clean out the attic, and so on. Just because we refuse to do these things, that doesn't mean they don't need to get done! Procrastinating does nothing more than delay the inevitable.

INTERRUPTIONS

You would think that interruptions would do little to cause you to waste time. After all, when the interruption is over you can simply go back to what you were doing, right?

In reality, interruptions can interfere with time management in a few ways. One is that we lose our train of thought. When we're interrupted and then return to our work, we often need to review where we were and what we were thinking at the time. We need to remind ourselves of the direction in which we were headed. Sometimes we even forget what we were trying to accomplish altogether!

Interruptions can also mean losing interest in the task at hand and this can mean putting it off. What we thought we would accomplish today gets put on the back burner because something else has come up, and soon we just don't care to continue at all.

Lack Of Goals

Sometimes a person does not spend their time effectively because they're not sure what they should be doing with that time. Without clear goals in mind, it's easy to simply waste away the hours of one's life doing little to accomplish anything - because you don't even know what you want to accomplish.

Goals can be personal or professional, and big or small. Having them in mind means knowing where you want to be in the future, and can also help you to see the things you need to do to get there. For example, if one goal is to save so much money for retirement, you know that you need to keep your finances in order now and need to see how much you're saving every month. If a smaller goal is to clean out your attic, you may know that this means buying some garbage bags and

24

storage bins and setting aside time every week to tackle that project.

When you lack goals it's easy to lack focus. Without focus you have no idea how you should be spending your time, which in turn means you accomplish nothing.

No Prioritizing

Lack of prioritizing skills is something like lacking goals in that you don't know what should occupy the time you have for maximum effectiveness. You have many different demands on your time and failure to realize which should come first and which should come last, and which should be dropped from your schedule altogether, can mean wasting that precious time.

Not prioritizing with your schedule can be compared to not prioritizing with your finances. If you buy new clothes without paying your rent, you have your priorities confused. If you go out drinking with your friends or go gambling rather than sending in a car payment, of course your priorities are off!

Learning how to set priorities may mean learning how to say no to certain projects or demands. This can be difficult especially for those that are not used to turning down requests and demands on their time, but like other time management skills, it can be done.

Delegating

Do you delegate your work, whether that's work in the office or work at home? If you have a difficult time with this, you're certainly not alone.

Many struggle with assigning work or sharing responsibilities, and for various reasons. It might be that they feel they're the only ones that can handle the work, they nitpick and criticize the work of others, they think others will look down on them if they share their responsibilities, or they just don't know how to ask for help.

Whatever the reason, taking on too much usually means that something if not everything will suffer. It also means that the things that are important to you may not be cared for since there is little room in your schedule for them.

All of these different time wasters and time bandits are very common for many. No doubt you've noticed yourself in some of these scenarios. And if so, what then? How can you address these situations so that you can maximize your time and really call it your own?

Let's go over each of these circumstances individually so you can understand how to address them and reclaim your time.

How To Overcome Procrastination

Everyone procrastinates; it can happen in short bursts, where you ignore the dirty dishes until bedtime, or it can be long-term such as when you put off quitting smoking until that terrible diagnosis comes back from your doctor.

Putting off or procrastinating unpleasant tasks and chores is only natural; we don't want to do something, so we don't. This can make us feel more in control, it can seem like a slight indulgence to walk away from unpleasant tasks, or we can simply ignore that thing we don't want to think about or handle at the moment.

Very often procrastination is something that is remedied after a short amount of time. Those dirty dishes eventually get done. The laundry gets folded or the gutters get cleaned out. We may also eventually find other solutions to the problem, such as having one of the kids do the dishes or paying someone else to clean out the gutters.

But there are many times when procrastination becomes a complete time waster. It may interfere with small goals but with larger ones as well. If you procrastinate when it comes to learning how to prepare healthy meals and procrastinate when it's time to go grocery shopping, your larger goal of losing weight is sidelined. This might also interfere with your goal of saving money since it may mean eating out more often, which is typically more expensive. So you not only need to scramble to find something to eat every day, you also put off those other goals as well.

As we've already mentioned, once time is gone, it's gone for good. So the time you use up procrastinating is not going to be given back to you. This too is another important reason to think about how procrastinating is an enemy of maximizing your schedule to accomplish your goals and take control of your life.

But this is easier said than done. Simply saying, "Get up and do this," isn't enough to motivate most people to stop procrastinating. If it were, no one would fall prey to this habit!

So how do you face your procrastination and overcome it? There are some things to consider. Let's go over those here.

MANAGEABLE STEPS

Often one reason people procrastinate is because they get overwhelmed with a project. If you need to clean out your attic, you may stand and look at those mounds of junk and realize it will take hours to get through everything ... and so you go and hit the couch instead.

There are many projects and goals that are overwhelming like this, and giving in to procrastination is all too easy when this happens. To avoid this, it's good to break things down into manageable steps. If you are facing just one manageable and workable step at a time, you're less likely to avoid it.

Here are some suggestions for how to

break down projects into manageable steps.

MAKE A LIST

You can't attack your projects step by step if you don't know what those steps are! If you make a list of everything that needs to get done, this can help tremendously.

Many steps are simple and some need steps within steps. For instance, if you want to adopt a child you know that your finances need to be in order for this to happen. You will then need to write up the steps needed to accomplish this.

There may be some chores where you don't necessarily need a list, such as cleaning out that attic, but there are other ways to avoid procrastination for those projects.

MANAGEABLE TIME

Your particular project may or may not have necessary steps, but in either case you can avoid procrastination by tackling it with manageable time. This means you should set aside a small amount of time to address the project, rather than trying to get everything done at once.

For example, suppose you need to clean out your attic. Set aside fifteen minutes every day to work at it. Do your cleaning for no less than this time; set a timer if necessary. If you're facing only fifteen minutes of cleaning work, you're much less likely to avoid it.

Setting a time limit can work with just about any project you have, although of course larger projects will mean more time, more often. To get your finances in order you may need to spend an hour this Saturday going through your bills and expenses and working up a reasonable budget. You may then need to spend another hour next week speaking with a debt consolidation company over the phone.

Another hour in their office may mean getting that consolidation loan. You may then need to spend a half hour every week going through the money you've spent that week, recording it and making sure your bills are paid on time. You also need to spend time regularly reviewing your budget to keep yourself on track.

But you'll note for these things too how every step is broken down into manageable timeframes. The key is to think solely about the next step, not about every single thing you need to get done to accomplish your task.

REMEMBER YOUR GOALS

To overcome procrastination, you should also remember your goals. Why are you doing this particular thing? What do you hope to accomplish? What will the end result look like?

Concentrating on the end product will mean you're taking your mind off the unpleasant task at hand. If your mind can focus on the end result it will not be so focused on the distraction of what you're doing now.

You can help yourself by making a list or writing out those goals or end results. For some, you can even cut out pictures in magazines or use other visual aids. If you're procrastinating when it comes to diet and exercise, find pictures of those with great physiques and keep them handy. If you procrastinate when it comes to cleaning out your basement or attic, find pictures of nicely organized rooms and have them in front of you constantly.

You can even purchase small items that remind you of your goals. Suppose you're procrastinating about organizing your finances but you know you must to save for retirement, when you plan on spending your days fishing. Buy a nice fishing rod and put it in a corner of your office so you remember why you're working on your checkbook.

When you keep yourself focused on what's ahead of you and not what's in front of you, then you can be better able to overcome the procrastination that's keeping you from properly managing and maximizing your time.

Just Do It

This phrase isn't just a Nike slogan; it's also a good piece of advice when you're procrastinating. Very often people wait until they "want" to do something or "feel like" doing something before they even begin. But this means just more procrastination! Chances are you'll never "want" to go back to school or "feel like" cleaning out the attic or getting on the treadmill, which means you may never do these things.

So instead, don't wait until your feelings are in order before you begin. Don't wait until you feel impelled or motivated. Instead, just get up and do it. Shut out your mind if you must, use music to get you going, daydream about something else if appropriate. Do whatever you need to do to get yourself off the couch and working toward your goal. Just don't wait for something else to get you moving!

Using these excuses of not feeling like doing something or not wanting to do something can mean putting that thing off indefinitely, so keep this in mind as well. What makes you think you'll feel like doing it tomorrow or will be motivated to do something next week? Chances are that just won't happen, so don't wait for it to happen. Just get up and start doing!

LIMITING YOUR INTERRUPTIONS

Interruptions are just a fact of the world in which we live. Very often someone else's business or concerns cannot wait until we are done and ready for them. Add to that are the interruptions by those who do not know we're busy and things that are not purposely meant to interrupt us at all. The ringing phone, a knock at the door, a growling stomach - all these interruptions must be accommodated.

But far too often there are interruptions that we allow to happen and to pull us away from our work or task at hand. And we may use that interruption as an excuse to put off what we were doing.

How do you stop interruptions? How can you get things done uninterrupted without being rude or neglecting other responsibilities and people as well? Consider a few quick points.

List Your Interruptions

What are common interruptions for you? There are some that are too trivial to list; a ringing phone, a knock at the door, and things like these are often too numerous to actually put on a list. But the reason you want to think about your common interruptions is that very often people allow certain interruptions to happen time and again. There are some which you can control and address, and some which are just inevitable. If you think about what you allow to interrupt you consistently, you can then face and address these effectively.

Ask yourself if any of these situations are common interruptions for you:

- Children who want attention.

- Computer games, browsing the internet.

- Friends and family that call on the phone to chat.

- A growling stomach.

- The urge to start a different project or take care of something other than the task at hand.

- Television programs.

- One's own boredom.

Think for a moment about how these

types of interruptions disrupt your train of thought and distract you from working effectively. Now think about how none of them are really important enough to be allowed to interrupt you! Often children interrupt when it's not necessary, or we eat out of boredom rather than because we're really hungry.

Consider carefully the things you consistently allow to interrupt your own work. Think of how many are unnecessary as well! So how to address these?

SCHEDULE TIME

One way you can avoid interruptions is by scheduling time when you are not to be interrupted. This can be something you tell others and something you tell yourself as well! If you set aside an hour to review some financial records for whatever reason, make it clear that family is not to interrupt you during this time. Turn off your cell phone and shut the door to your room. And don't allow yourself to wander away from your project as well.

You can prepare for this scheduled time by making sure everything is taken care of first. The children are fed and have supervision or other plans. You have a snack with you or have eaten. You don't have any other pressing projects that need tending so you can put those off for your scheduled time.

When you schedule time in which you should remain uninterrupted you know that you have no reason to do anything other than tend to the work at hand. There is no reason to entertain your children or to wander away for something to eat. Unless it's a dire emergency, that time should be treated as sacred.

You might need to get tough with yourself during this scheduled time as well. When you feel an urge to get up and do the dishes or tend to another chore, tell yourself that this isn't the time to do that. Your time right now is scheduled just as if you were at work or the doctor's office or were sitting in church. You don't handle other tasks when you're doing these things, so don't try to handle something else when you're scheduled to take care of chores or responsibilities.

TUNE OUT

Another way to avoid needless interruption is to tune out. This means no television, MP3 player, food, and anything else when you're working on a particular project. Close the blinds if you tend to stare out the window. Keep the pets out of the room in which you're working.

While some background music may work in some situations, even having that can mean constantly changing the channel or skipping songs. You then realize the battery on your MP3 player is low and it needs to be plugged in ... and while you're up you may as well get a soda from the fridge ... and while you're in the kitchen you should probably do these dishes ... and so on. If you find that you cannot keep background music on without being interrupted, give that up as well.

You may also need to be brutally honest with yourself in this regard. How often do you keep the cell phone on or have the television running because you want to be interrupted from your project? When something is boring or tedious or otherwise annoying it's easy to allow an interruption so that we don't need to keep working on that boring project. And then we don't need to take the blame ourselves for not keeping up with it! After all, it was mom that called on the phone or the interesting news story that distracted us, so it's not really our fault, right?

Tuning out is necessary in order to avoid interruption and to get the job at hand done. Remember this when you're tempted to keep the television running or want to listen to music or do something else while trying to concentrate on one particular task.

COMMUNICATE

Another way to handle interruptions is to communicate clearly with those that may be interrupting you. For many, it's difficult to tell your children or friends or someone else that you cannot be interrupted right now. But you need to learn how to do this so you don't allow interruptions to take over your schedule.

Usually it's good to let someone know that you cannot be interrupted right now, but can make time for them later. If your children interrupt when you're working, tell them that you'll talk to them after dinner. If your mother calls while you're trying to get that attic cleaned out, tell her that you'll call back in two hours.

If you make an appointment with someone to take care of something then they won't be put off or hurt by the fact that you're not dropping everything right at the moment. This will also keep the immediate interruption from becoming a large interruption. It's much easier to quickly put off someone and return to your task at hand than it is to take the time they need for their concerns, and then try to return to your work.

In some cases, you can even tell someone why you need to put them off. Try saying, "Unfortunately I'm right in the middle of a project right now and can't step away. Can I get back with you before the end of the day?" When someone knows you're putting them off for a good reason, they are less likely to be upset or offended.

Remember that an interruption will turn into a major distraction only if you allow it to. If there is nothing critical about your interruption and it can be put off, get into the habit of doing just that.

SETTING GOALS TO

MAXIMIZE YOUR TIME

As mentioned, one reason that many fail to maximize their time is that they just don't know how. Time should be used to accomplish things, but what? And how? Without clear goals in mind it's easy to simply fritter away time and then wonder why you're not where you want to be in life.

Chances are you know what you want and know where you want to be, but have never really solidified or cemented these desires into real dreams and goals. That wishful thinking and daydreaming will do nothing to get you there! Making those goals concrete and figuring how to work toward them will mean making the best use of your time in order to achieve everything you want.

SETTING GOALS

So what are your goals? You probably want to break them down into personal and professional goals, if you work or have a career. These goals can also be large or small, immediate and long-term.

Here are some suggestions for considering your goals, both personal and professional:

- Losing weight, even if it's just ten pounds; exercising more, or stopping smoking.

- Adopting a child.

- Getting an advanced degree.

- Getting a promotion or a better job.

- Running your own business.

- Starting an online business or website.

- Buying a vacation home.

- Saving "X" amount of money for retirement.

- Organizing your finances, your dresser drawers, your basement, and so on.

- Investigating a consolidation loan to handle your credit card and other debt.

- Selling your home and buying a new one.

Think about your own goals; give them a real voice. Write them down one by one; leave none of them out, even the small goals. If necessary, walk through your home as this may remind you of different goals you have. Your office may remind of you the career goals you have, or remind you that you would like to try to sell things online.

GOALS WITHIN GOALS

As with most projects and jobs, it's easy to get overwhelmed with reaching goals because they require so much work and effort. Often you cannot just make one change or do one thing and suddenly you've reached your goal. Typically there are other steps to the process that need to be considered.

You may call these goals within goals, and you need to note them as well. Every step that should be taken needs to be considered; this is how you can make a plan for how to reach your goals.

As an example, suppose you want to exercise more. This will mean reviewing your schedule and removing unnecessary distractions from your time. Rather than being on the company bowling league every Tuesday, you'll use that night to hit the gym. Your weekly poker game will become a monthly game so you can exercise more during those other nights.

Goals within goals are also those manageable steps we've discussed which help a person to not be overwhelmed. This is necessary with goals because of course they often mean a lot of work, whether they're small goals or large ones. Losing weight means learning to cook healthier meals, making a grocery list every week, setting aside time to pack a healthy lunch, and actually getting off the couch and on the treadmill. Each of these can and should be broken down into manageable steps so that you don't get overwhelmed and just give up on your goals.

SCHEDULE AND PLANNING

To maximize your time to reach your goals, you'll need to use some scheduling and planning. This is where many people fail to reach their goals; they know what they want and may know what is needed to achieve it, but actually going out and doing those things is something completely different.

Putting the steps to your goals in logical order will help with your scheduling and planning. To get that advanced degree, of course you need to investigate what classes you'll need to take and when they're scheduled, and if you can afford them before you rearrange your schedule to get to class. To run an online business, you need to investigate the products you wish to sell and learn how online selling really works before you just put up a website and assume you'll get orders.

When your goals are in logical steps, then it's time to schedule and plan for them. This may mean some sacrifice on your part as you give up other plans in your schedule in order to work in those things you want to work at.

As you schedule and plan, think about what you can do this week, this month, in the next few months, and so on. What can you accomplish this week to work toward your goal? What will you do next week? What will you accomplish before this month is over?

You'll also need to make concrete plans when you schedule in the steps of your goal. Rather than saying "this week" you'll meet with a college counselor about classes needed for your degree, choose a specific day or night. Write these things in your calendar as you would any other obligation you have.

Track Progress

To keep yourself reaching toward your goals, it's good to track your progress as you go. You can mark off items from lists, see the end results from things you have already done, and reward yourself along the way.

As you set manageable goals within goals, make up a rewards system or a way to track your progress. As you reach one milestone, give yourself a small treat or reward. Remind yourself of how far you've come.

If you look behind you and see your own progress, you won't be so discouraged about what is in front of you when it comes to what you still need to accomplish. Continue to remind yourself that everything is accomplished in small steps and that you'll continue to achieve as you go along. In this way you won't be tempted to give in to discouragement as you see those goals still somewhat far off.

Celebrate each milestone of your goal along the way. If you do this you'll stay on track and make the most use of your time.

SETTING PRIORITIES FOR YOUR SCHEDULE

What are your priorities in your schedule? If you aren't sure or assume you have none, you may want to think again. Most people have priorities but they don't realize it. If you would never leave the house without a shower, you are making hygiene a priority. If you never fail to get your children their breakfast and make their lunches before they go to school, then caring for them is a priority. When you go to work every day, your job is a priority.

Often we take care of things that are a priority without even realizing it or considering them as such. We just do them automatically because we know they need to get done; this means they're a priority.

While work and children and hygiene and household chores and things such as these obviously should be a priority, it's amazing how often someone will allow something else to become a priority when perhaps it should instead take a backseat.

Let's look at some common examples of this so you can understand what happens when priorities get confused.

RECREATION

Everyone needs recreation and relaxation; without it, people get nervous, anxious, stressed, and overly tired. Recreation can also stimulate the imagination and strengthen bonds between people as they spend time together.

Talking about priorities does not mean that you should never indulge in recreation or just rest. However, there is a problem when it becomes more of a priority than working toward your goals, or when you indulge in it so often that you're left with little time to do other things.

And recreation doesn't need to necessarily mean going to the bar or going out to play tennis with friends. It can also mean watching television, surfing the internet, reading, engaging in hobbies, walking around the mall, working on cars, talking to friends on the phone, and so on. When these things begin to interfere with your specific plans or goals, or when they monopolize your time or are being done far too often, then they've taken a priority with you.

Time Wasters And Distractions

Along with recreation, we may allow things that waste our time and that do nothing but distract us to become a priority. For instance, when shopping for something new for the home we may research a few options and decide what is best. But then we have the urge to research every single option we have and to research these things well past the point of necessity. We may think that this should be a priority because we want to know all our choices, but chances are we're just wasting time with useless information.

Other distractions might be hobbies and pursuits that have no real purpose and which we have no need for in the first place. We decide one day that we love interior decorating and start learning all about it, with no real intent of pursuing it as a career. This priority has now wasted valuable time that could have been used to research something that really matters and that would really contribute to our life overall.

OTHER PEOPLE

When do other people become a priority and when should they be put off? There's no easy answer to that as there are times when other people should take priority over what we want to do. A sick child or family member, a friend going through a crisis, and even volunteer work may be a priority and with good reason.

Typically however we allow others to become a priority over ourselves when there really is no reason for that to happen. Children need attention and to be cared for but they also need to respect an adult's time as well and can often entertain themselves. As they get older of course they should be taking care of many of their own needs such as making food or doing laundry.

When thinking of other people and how their needs take priority over our plans for our schedule, it's good to consider if we're really responding to a friend in crisis or just to someone's need for attention. Your friend is bored and so he or she calls you up. If you can schedule in recreation then there's nothing wrong with that but just dropping everything you're doing because they ask means they're taking a top priority.

Other people may take a priority whenever they ask something of you. Your church needs a volunteer and you automatically sign up. Your boss wants to know if someone can take on an extra project and you say yes without even really thinking about it. Whatever anyone else asks, you just automatically do without a second thought.

People can become a priority when we allow their demands to come first, when there is no real reason to do this. They may also become a priority if we allow them to interrupt, to distract us, to tell us that our goals will never be reached, or to discourage us in any way. Their thinking and their needs take priority over our own and this is not the way to maximize one's time.

How To Set Priorities

So how do you set priorities? Obviously you cannot just stop working or give up on taking care of the children or your home in order to maximize your time. There will always be priorities in your schedule that are set by someone else or that simply need to be cared for because of their nature.

The key here is how a person spends their time when it comes to circumstances over which they have a choice. You have a choice as to how much recreation you have every week. You have a choice as to whether or not you'll volunteer for your child's school project or sit on the phone for an hour while your friend drones on and on.

YOUR PRIORITIES

One thing to remember about priorities is that you may let other people set those for you, and you may be allowing their priorities to overshadow yours. When you take on a volunteer project for your child's school, this is a priority for your child, his or her teacher, and the school. But is it your priority? When you take up a volunteer project through church or a civic organization, is this something really important to you or is it more important to these other people?

This can happen too with recreation.

Is going out with friends really something you enjoy and get the most out of, or is it more of a priority for them? Are you going because you've always gone or feel obligated? When a friend or your mom calls and talks on the phone for an hour, how important is this conversation to you? Are you perhaps allowing what's important to someone else to become important to you, more so than your real goals?

If you can keep these thoughts in mind when you set your priorities and keep your calendar, you'll realize how your own important tasks and goals need to come first and how to set the work of others on the back burner.

Schedule And Calendar

A good schedule is going to be necessary in order to set priorities and stick with them. Go over your calendar and see where your priorities have fallen; if you have no time in your calendar to work toward what is important to you, but find that you're always doing for other people, then you've lost sight of your own priorities.

When something is a priority for you, it makes its way onto your calendar whether you realize it or not. Every morning when you go to work, your job has become a priority on your calendar. When you shower, make dinner, go grocery shopping, and do all these things without even considering them, they have time and space on your calendar even if you don't necessarily write them down.

Letting your own priorities slip will mean that you now need to work them into your calendar and your schedule, even writing them down if necessary. On Tuesday night you'll be in school getting your advanced degree no matter what, every weekend you're going for a job on Saturday afternoon no matter what, and so on.

Scheduling means omitting some things that should not be a priority for you and adding in those things that should be. Once you realize your own priorities and realize how you've let other people and their concerns take precedence over yours, then this will be much easier for you.

Learning To Delegate

How often do you delegate tasks in order to get done the things you want to get done? There may be many things that cannot and should not be delegated. Your children need attention from you as does your spouse or partner. When at work there are things that you simply must do yourself as you have no other options. You might not be able to afford to pay someone to clean your house, care for your lawn, do your laundry, and so on.

But often delegating can be done in many ways that you wouldn't imagine. And if you delegate some tasks this means opening up your schedule so that you can work toward those goals you have.

Let's take a look at some ways you can delegate tasks at home and on the job so that you can maximize your time.

IN THE FAMILY

It's a sad fact that even career women today still wind up doing the majority share of the housework, child raising, and chores caring for the home. Whatever the reason for this, it's good for the entire family to consider how things can and should be delegated so that chores are shared more equally.

Here are some examples of how this can happen:

•   If both adults in the home work, why must mom always make dinner? Assign nights when your husband or partner will prepare dinner completely. Or trade off -

one will make dinner if the other gets the children their breakfast in the morning and prepares their lunches for the day.

• You can also trade off other chores. One cooks but the other does dishes. One does laundry each week and the other cleans the house.

• Trade days when you run errands or take the children to school.

• As children get older, they can and should be helping out around the house as well. Younger children can set and clear the table, bring their dirty clothes to the laundry room, and pick up their own toys. Older children can do yard work, housework, cooking, making their own lunch, laundry, and chores such as these.

It may take a few family meetings, a chore chart, or other methods to get everyone on board but it can and should be done. Not only will delegating tasks in the home free up your time, it will also teach everyone responsibility and keep any one person from being overwhelmed as well.

AT HOME

As the family pitches in and you delegate responsibility to others, there may be additional ways you can delegate chores and jobs. While you might not be able to afford a full-time household staff, there are more affordable ways to get help and to delegate at home.

•	Neighborhood children can help with yard work, walking a dog, or even house cleaning. You may even know someone from your church or religious organization that would be very affordable when it comes to this type of help.

•	If there is a college nearby, even a community college, you may be able to advertise the help you need around the home and the price you're willing to pay. Often college students are willing to do small chores or babysitting for an affordable price.

•	If you're caring for an aging parent or disabled spouse or child, you may be able to have a visiting nurse or home health aide visit on a regular basis. This may be reimbursed through your insurance, Medicare or Medicaid.

•	Other family members should also be pitching in when it comes to aging spouses or family that needs care. Your own siblings, aunts and uncles, and other relatives can and should help with these situations.

If you put your mind to it you may find that there are many ways you can get help around the house and delegate certain chores and tasks without spending a fortune on professional help. However, you may also want to consider if the price you pay for a professional is worth the time you save as well. A cleaning company, a professional lawn care service, or someone to tutor your child and assist with homework can be worth the few dollars you pay if it means getting your time back in exchange.

At Work

Can you delegate chores and tasks at work? Sometimes the answer is legitimately no; there are reasons why you must do certain jobs on your own. Others may not be qualified and these things may just be your job to do. But chances are you can find ways to delegate tasks at work so that you are using your time effectively there as well.

For example, can you have someone from the clerical staff help you with minor typing or filing? Can someone return basic phone calls for you? Is it possible to teach someone, such as the receptionist, some basic responsibilities of your paperwork so that he or she can handle these things for you?

There might also be times when you do have staff on hand that can assist with different responsibilities but you're hesitant to have them do this. You may not trust their work or just don't know how to speak up. In any event, delegating at work will mean getting the most out of the time you do have so that projects are completely properly and effectively.

Why You Don't Delegate

If you still have a difficult time thinking of ways to delegate, whether at home or in the office, you may want to consider why this is. Many people hesitate to ask for help or to assign work to others for a variety of reasons. Let's look at some common ones and consider if any of them may apply to you.

- You assume that no one can do a job

as well as you do, or you nitpick the work of others.

• You may feel that if you don't do things yourself, others will look down on you.

• You're simply used to taking on all chores and responsibilities by yourself and have a hard time asking for help or giving up work to another person.

• You are often made to feel guilty if you don't take on extra responsibilities and chores.

• You enjoy the rush and pressure of trying to do too much.

While it may be uncomfortable, especially at first, for you to start delegating tasks, it's going to be necessary to learn this habit and skill in order to maximize your time. When you begin to hesitate to pass along responsibility, consider a few points:

• Children need to learn responsibility and how to care for themselves and the home. It's better for them to have chores around the house than not, so giving them age appropriate work is good for them as well as for you.

•   If both parents work outside the home, why would one do the majority of the housework, child raising, and so on? This can be damaging to one's health if someone were to get overworked and frazzled.

•   Allowing someone else to have responsibility can build their self-esteem and self-confidence. They can also feel appreciated and part of a team, such as at the office.

•   If you're overly critical of the work of others and assume you're the only one that can handle certain responsibilities, might this be a reflection of an ego out of control? Why is your way better or "right"?

•   When you assume that others will look down on you if you don't take on everything yourself, might this be untrue? How do you know what others are thinking? And is their thinking more important than the goals and plans you have for yourself and the ways you want to maximize your time?

Delegating may be something of a skill but it is one you can learn. Often it gets easier along the way. Keep reminding yourself that you have better things to do with your time than trying to do everything in front of you, and that you will accomplish more if you think of quality projects you want to care for, not just the quantity of projects.

Your Time Is Yours

With all this information we've shared so far, what would you say is the most important point when it comes to maximizing your time?

No doubt the idea that time is limited is important. When you understand this, you realize how you should never fritter it away. It becomes most valuable and something you need to guard and protect.

Or perhaps you're realizing how you should never let another person's priorities take precedence over your own. When you do, you're allowing them to steal your time just as you would allow someone to steal your money. As you learn to make your own priorities a, well, a priority, you learn how to set your schedule and your calendar so that your time is used wisely.

There are many good points we've made so far about time and how to spend it. We've also covered many points regarding how you should view time and the things you do to fill it.

But one very important point to consider above and beyond all others is that your time is your own. It's belongs to you, not to your boss, your family, your friends or anyone else.

You might immediately argue with this, saying that when you're at work, your time does belong to your boss. Or that you do need to spend time to care for your children. This is all true to a certain extent; your boss does have the right to tell you how you'll spend at work and having children, a relationship, a home, and friends and family will all mean demands on your time.

But the bottom line is that you choose to dedicate your time to these things. You choose to have a job with a boss that tells you what to do. Those hours during the day are yours and you can easily sit at home and refuse to work, but you choose to devote them to a job. Those hours you spend with your children are yours, but you've chosen to give them away to your children - and rightly so.

Realizing that your time is your own to keep or give away as you please should help you to understand all the finer points of maximizing your time. When someone interrupts and you step away from your project, you have now chosen to give away your time to them. That's your time to do with as you please, so it's up to you to make that decision. When someone else's concerns take priority over yours, you've chosen to give away that time that is yours to their needs.

Of course there are times when this is a good thing; no one is saying that you should suddenly become selfish and do only what you want, when you want, all the time. If you decide to have children then it could be said that you owe them a debt of time since they need attention from you, both physically and emotionally. So does your partner and your friends as well.

And certainly giving away your time to others has its own advantages. You give your boss eight or nine hours every day in exchange for that paycheck you get every week. This in turn means you have a home in which to live, food to eat, and so on. Your time has become a tradeoff with benefits to you, not just the other person.

This is true in personal relationships as well. If you tradeoff your time to give some to friends, you have strong bonds with them in return. They'll be there for you when you need someone to talk with or when you want to go out and have a few laughs. You give time to your partner and in return have a loving relationship. Giving your time in these ways will benefit you.

But again, you're making a choice. There are many people out there that choose a different course of action. They're indifferent to the time needed to invest in a relationship or the time children need in order to grow and mature properly. Often this selfishness of refusing to give up one's time has very poor results for everyone.

It is important however to strike a balance in what you give away when it comes to time and what you keep for yourself. No one can force you to give your time away; the only thing anyone can do is put a choice in front of you, and then you need to make that choice for yourself. Your job puts a choice in front of you for either earning a living or sponging off someone else, so you choose to go into work every day. Having children means a choice of dedicating some time with them in exchange for a strong family life or seeing

your children be neglected and no doubt
developing behavior problems because of
this. Your time is yours and every minute
of every day you choose how you'll spend it.

Your Responsibility

One reason it's so important to
understand that your time is your own is
because we all need to take responsibility
for how we spend that time. It's too easy
to think that you're not getting anything
done because your friends interrupt on the
phone, the children are a top priority, you
need to handle everything on your own, and
so on.

But in reality, you make a choice to
talk to your friend on the phone when he or
she calls, don't you? You've made a choice
to devote every waking minute to your
children rather than prioritizing and sharing
responsibilities. You make a choice to take
on all jobs and responsibilities yourself,
rather than delegating.

It's true that often someone else can
be very good at making a person feel bad if
they don't give up their time, but in this
area too it's good to take responsibility for
your own feelings. You can't allow someone

else to use guilt or manipulation to force you to give up your time, not unless you've made a choice to do so.

When you start to take responsibility for your own time, realizing that it's yours to do with as you please, you understand better how to maximize your time. You better understand that you are making a choice when you allow someone else to take that time away from you.

Making Choices

Choosing how you spend your time is like choosing how you spend your money. Your money is yours to do with as you please. You may again be arguing, saying that your money must go to the mortgage or rent, car payment, utilities, and so on. But as with your time, you're making a choice to spend your money on these things. You're choosing to live in a home or apartment and have chosen on with the payment it has. You choose to have a car and utilities rather than to be homeless and trying to live off the land.

And when someone asks you for money, what is your response? Chances are you think carefully about how much you give away and to whom. You probably don't just pull out your wallet and spread around your money to anyone and everyone that asks.

Your time is much the same. When someone tries to interrupt or wants you to give up your priorities for theirs, you need to think about this carefully. Again, this isn't to say that you never give your time to someone else but you should do so because you've made a careful choice. You've measured their needs for your time versus your wants for your time and have decided on what to do; you haven't just given your time away blindly.

If you begin to think of your time as being much like your money, you may realize the value it has. You may realize that indeed it is yours to do with as you please. The decisions you make regarding your time should be made carefully and considerately.

THE TIME FOR ACTION IS NOW!

So how can you apply all these tips and tricks we've outlined in order to maximize your time and achieve your goals? There is no clear-cut answer that will work for everyone, but there are some additional points you can consider in order to get you on your way. Think of the following:

SMALL STEPS

Trying to maximize your time and change bad habits all at once is rarely effective. Typically you need to take small steps to apply everything we've outlined so far. How to do this?

• Pick one thing you need to work on. This might be delegating, prioritizing, tuning out from distractions, or something else. Work on it this week and the next.

Get

• into the habit of applying the tips we've outlined for that particular issue. When you are more skilled with that, move on to another point.

• When working on a project remember the tips we've outlined regarding taking small steps for that as well. Work on something for 15 minutes every day or every other day. Set aside one hour on the weekend rather than thinking you'll spend your entire Saturday cleaning out the garage or organizing your finances.

• Be patient with yourself. As you make progress, realize that you won't change everything at once. Be glad when you conquer one small step or overcome one obstacle.

REMEMBER YOUR GOALS

Another good reason to write down your goals is so that you can keep them in front of you constantly. Think of the things you want to accomplish by organizing your time and making the most out of it. Do you want to lose weight? Do you want to clean and organize your house from top to bottom? Do you want that advanced degree or better career? Do you just want to be more organized with your life overall?

Remembering the things you want to do with your time will help to impel you to keep up with the changes necessary to maximize your schedule. Think seriously about how you'll feel when you finally have a workable schedule and can then pursue those goals. Imagine all the benefits of achieving the things you want to achieve - having lost weight, having cleaned your house or gotten control of your debt, having gotten that degree, and so on.

When things get difficult and you get tempted to give up on your plans for maximizing your time, and that television is calling, think seriously about your goals. Think about what you're trying to accomplish and the benefits you'll see.

TRACK YOUR PROGRESS

As you move along with maximizing your time to achieve your goals, it's good to keep track of your progress. This means you can be encouraged to continue along, as you see how you've made changes and how those changes have impacted you.

When you look back and see progress you've made then you know you're on the right track. You know that you're being effective and are accomplishing your goals and maximizing your time. Knowing that you're on the right track can help you to stay on that track.

As said, it's good to reward yourself along the way. Mark milestones in your calendar and be sure to acknowledge and celebrate them. This can be with something as simple as a long hot bath or it can mean a new outfit, a new power tool, a long romantic weekend, or just an hour to yourself as you contemplate your own progress.

When you reward yourself and acknowledge your progress you really drive home the point that taking control of your time and your schedule is a good thing. It means good things for you and your family. There are reasons why you're doing this and those reasons are ones that should be celebrated.

GIVE YOURSELF A BREAK

Far too often, someone trying to maximize their time and organize their schedule will make the mistake of thinking that every moment needs to be scheduled and that every minute of recreation is a waste. In reality, people need rest and relaxation on a regular basis. Being able to shut out complicated matters from the mind and allow it to have some "brain candy" every now and again can mean less stress.

Hobbies can also indulge one's imagination and creativity and even sharpen memory skills and problems solving abilities. When you do crossword puzzles or read, you are strengthening those connections in the brain that allow for clear thinking.

Taking a break can mean strengthening bonds between friends and family as well. Being able to laugh over drinks with friends or go to the zoo with the children means feeling closer to those people. Time spent with a spouse or parents or siblings or close friends is important for everyone involved.

Being unbalanced with recreation and wastes of time is bad for your schedule in both ways; too much recreation and you get nothing done, but no recreation and you create stress and tension for yourself. You can also make other people feel bad if you constantly turn them down for recreation opportunities, and this includes your spouse, children, and family.

TIME IS LIMITED

To really motivate you to make the most of your time, you can also remember that time is limited for everyone. This isn't meant to be morbid or depressing; this is simply a reality that needs to be considered. When you waste a minute or a day, you'll never get it back.

It's also good to remember that time will continue to move forward no matter how you spend it. Soon enough it will be a year from now, and then five years from now. And will you have accomplished something in that time or not? Will you still be right where you are today or will you be closer to achieving your goals?

Understanding that time is limited will mean that you'll make the most of it, no matter what. When something that is not a priority for you begins to eat up your time, you'll see that time as being too precious and valuable to waste that way. You won't let someone steal it from you anymore than you would allow someone to steal money from your wallet.

Maximizing your time will take practice and it might be a bit uncomfortable at first as you learn how to say "no" to people and start putting yourself first. But it's a skill that can and will be learned. It's something you must consider in order to be sure you're making the most of it.

And the time to start doing that is now! Right now, today. After all, today's time is part of that "bank" of time you have and should be thought of as being just as valuable as any other time you'll get.

So what have you done today to maximize your time? Going over these points is a good start, but unless you start applying them, you'll never get past that good start. So don't put it off; do everything you can today to start maximizing your time and making the most of your schedule, and by doing so you'll get the most out of your life!

Made in the USA
Lexington, KY
04 August 2011